WEREWOLVES!

MARK CHEATHAM

PowerKiDS press

New York

Published in 2012 by The Rosen Publishing Group, Inc.
29 East 21st Street, New York, NY 10010

First Edition

Editor: Joanne Randolph
Book Design: Planman Technologies
Illustrations: Planman Technologies

Library of Congress Cataloging-in-Publication Data
Cheatham, Mark.
 Werewolves! / by Mark Cheatham. — 1st ed.
    p. cm. — (Jr. graphic monster stories)
 Includes index.
 ISBN 978-1-4488-6220-7 (library binding) — ISBN 978-1-4488-6399-0 (pbk.)
 — ISBN 978-1-4488-6400-3 (6-pack)
 1. Werewolves—Juvenile literature. I. Title.
 GR830.W4C54 2012
 398.24'54—dc23
                                          2011022439

Manufactured in the United States of America
CPSIA Compliance Information: Batch #PLW2102PK: For Further Information contact Rosen Publishing, New York, New York at 1-800-237-9932

Contents

Main Characters

Jeanne Boulet (1750-1764) The first person officially recorded as having been killed by the Beast of Gévaudan.

Jean Chastel (1708-1789) Killed the Beast of Gévaudan in June, 1767.

Marquis d'Apcher (1745-1798) French nobleman who organized a massive hunt for the Beast of Gévaudan that resulted in the beast's death in 1767.

Antoine de Beauterne Gunbearer to King Louis XV. He claimed to have killed the Beast of Gévaudan in 1765, though killings by the beast continued. Received rewards and public acclaim for killing the beast.

Captain Duhamel From 1764-until 1765, led a troop of light cavalry and groups of **peasants** in unsuccessful hunts for the Beast of Gévaudan.

King Louis XV (1710-1774) Sent royal troops and other resources to help protect Gévaudan from **attacks** by the beast.

Werewolves!

THREE CHILDREN CAMPED WITH THEIR GRANDFATHER IN THE LONELY WOODS.

THE OLDER BOY TRIED TO FRIGHTEN HIS BROTHER AND SISTER.

"MY GRANDFATHER LIVED IN GÉVAUDAN, A REGION IN SOUTHERN FRANCE. MOST PEOPLE THERE WERE SIMPLE, HARDWORKING FARMERS.

"TOWNS THROUGHOUT GÉVAUDAN WERE FULL OF PEOPLE DURING MARKET DAY.

"FROM THIS REGION OF SOUTHERN FRANCE CAME A STORY ABOUT A TERRIBLE BEAST, WHICH MANY PEOPLE BELIEVED WAS A WEREWOLF. THE STORY BEGINS WITH A YOUNG GIRL TENDING CATTLE IN A PASTURE."

ARRRRGH!

"A HUGE BEAST, UNLIKE ANY SEEN BEFORE, ATTACKED THE GIRL.

"LUCKILY FOR THE GIRL, THE BEAST FEARED THE BULLS."

HELP!

"THE BEAST RAN OFF, BUT THIS WAS JUST THE BEGINNING OF TWO YEARS OF **TERROR**.

7

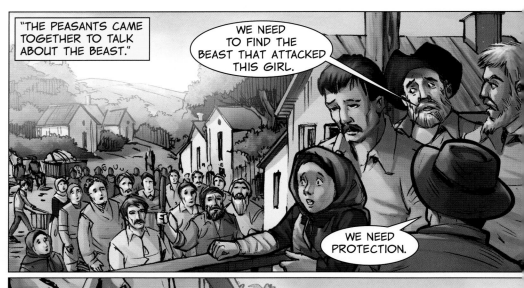

"A FEW DAYS LATER, A FARMER WAS WORKING IN HIS FIELDS."

WHAT IS THAT SOUND? IS THAT THE DOG?

"SUDDENLY, A **CREATURE** TOWERED OVER HIM."

LEAVE ME, DEVIL!

ARRRRGH!

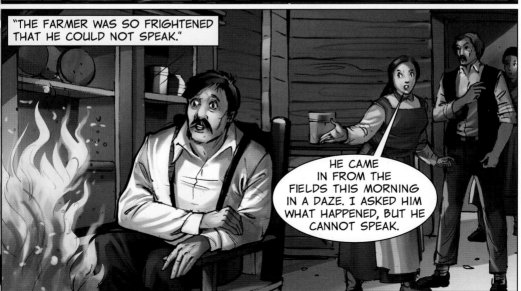

"THE FARMER WAS SO FRIGHTENED THAT HE COULD NOT SPEAK."

HE CAME IN FROM THE FIELDS THIS MORNING IN A DAZE. I ASKED HIM WHAT HAPPENED, BUT HE CANNOT SPEAK.

"THE ANGRY PEASANTS **VOWED** TO HUNT THE BEAST."

LET US HUNT IT NOW!

KILL THE BEAST!

KILL IT!

"THEY SEARCHED THE COUNTRYSIDE FOR MANY DAYS.

"THEY KILLED A FEW WOLVES. THEY COULD NOT FIND THE BEAST, THOUGH.

"THE ATTACKS CONTINUED. THE BEAST MOST OFTEN ATTACKED WOMEN AND CHILDREN. **FUNERALS** BECAME COMMON IN GÉVAUDAN.

"CAPTAIN DUHAMEL AND THE KING'S SOLDIERS CAME TO GÉVAUDAN TO HUNT THE BEAST.

"WHEN THEY THOUGHT THE BEAST WAS TRAPPED, IT WOULD DISAPPEAR."

THE BEAST IS *NOT* A WOLF!

"THE KILLINGS CONTINUED.

"THE PEASANTS LEARNED MORE ABOUT THE BEAST. IT HUNTED AT DAWN OR DUSK. IT KEPT LOW TO THE GROUND WHEN STALKING ITS **PREY**. IT THEN POUNCED LIKE A CAT.

"FARMERS HAD TO GUARD THEIR WIVES AND CHILDREN, SO THEIR CROPS WENT UNTENDED.

"VILLAGE MARKETS WERE EMPTY BECAUSE PEOPLE WERE AFRAID TO LEAVE THEIR HOMES.

"THE PEOPLE OF GÉVAUDAN PLEADED WITH THE FRENCH KING FOR HELP."

BECAUSE OF THE BEAST, WE LIVE IN FEAR.

MY ROYAL HUNTERS LED BY ANTOINE DE BEAUTERNE WILL GO TO GÉVAUDAN!

"DE BEAUTERNE STUDIED MAPS OF GÉVAUDAN, NOTING PLACES WHERE THE BEAST HAD KILLED. HE MADE CAREFUL PLANS FOR THE HUNT."

"DE BEAUTERNE AND HIS MEN WENT ON HUNTS EVERY DAY. THEY COULD NOT FIND THE BEAST.

"THE BEAST CONTINUED TO ATTACK. IT CARRIED OFF SMALL CHILDREN.

"SOMETIMES THE BEAST COULD BE MADE TO DROP ITS PREY.

"THE PEASANTS ASKED DE BEAUTERNE WHY HE HAD NOT KILLED THE BEAST AFTER SO MANY HUNTS. DE BEAUTERNE DECIDED THAT A LARGE WOLF WOULD BE EASIER TO FIND AND WOULD QUIET THE PEOPLE'S FEARS."

BOOM!

BOOM!

THE BEAST IS DEAD!

"SOME SAID THE DEAD WOLF WAS THE BEAST THAT ATTACKED THEM."

THAT IS THE BEAST!

"THE PEASANTS **PRAISED** DE BEAUTERNE. LATER, THE KING REWARDED HIM."

HERO OF GÉVAUDAN!

"WEEKS PASSED WITHOUT AN ATTACK, AND THEN THE BEAST KILLED AGAIN."

WE WERE TENDING THE SHEEP. THE BEAST SPRANG AT US FROM THE BUSHES! IT TOOK FRANCES!

"SOME SAID THE BEAST WAS A WEREWOLF, A MAN WHO BECAME A WOLF."

LADIES, MAY I ESCORT YOU?

"IN ANOTHER TIME, THEY MAY HAVE ACCEPTED A STRANGER'S OFFER. YET THE WOMEN WERE SHOCKED WHEN THEY NOTICED THE MAN'S HAND."

NO, THANK YOU, OUR HUSBANDS ARE COMING.

I WILL BE ON MY WAY THEN. BE CAREFUL NOW.

"THE PEASANTS CAME TOGETHER TO PRAY FOR HELP. THEY MARCHED TO AN **ANCIENT CHAPEL.**

"A HUNTER NAMED JEAN CHASTEL HAD HIS BULLETS AND GUN BLESSED BY THE PRIEST.

"THE BEAST ATTACKED A HERDSMAN. THE HERDSMAN LIVED AND REPORTED THAT THE BEAST WAS NEARBY.

"A NOBLEMAN NAMED MARQUIS D'APCHER ORGANIZED A HUNT. A GROUP WOULD DRIVE THE BEAST THROUGH THE WOODS TO WHERE HUNTERS WAITED IN **AMBUSH**.

"THE MEN DROVE THE BEAST BEFORE THEM. JEAN CHASTEL WAITED AHEAD IN THE WOODS. HE READ HIS BIBLE AND PRAYED.

"SUDDENLY THE BEAST STOOD BEFORE CHASTEL."

BOOM!

"THE BEAST FELL DEAD BEFORE HIM."

BEAST, YOU WILL KILL NO MORE!

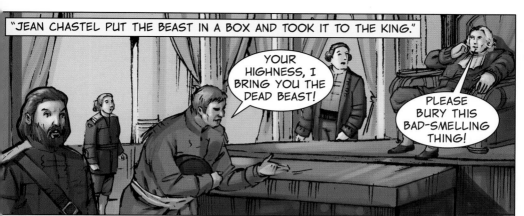

More Werewolf Stories

Wisconsin Werewolves In 1936, a man claimed to have seen a werewolf near Jefferson, Wisconsin. The creature was digging alongside the road. It was covered with hair and as tall as a man but had a muzzle like a wolf's. There were also sightings of the Wisconsin creature in 1964 and 1972.

Texas Werewolves In 1958, a woman near Greggton, Texas, observed a large, hairy figure with yellow eyes and a wolflike snout outside her bedroom window. She shined a flashlight on the bushes where it had disappeared. A moment later a man emerged from the bushes and ran off down the road.

Pennsylvania Werewolves In 1973, there were a number of reported sightings of a large, werewolflike creature. It was 6 to 7 feet (1.8–2 m) tall, completely covered with hair, and gave off a terrible odor.

Monster Facts

- Between 1764 and 1767, the Beast of Gévaudan in southern France is credited with killing as many as 100 people and injuring more than 30 others.

- According to legend, a human may become a werewolf by being bitten by a werewolf or by drinking water from a wolf's paw print. One can also become a werewolf by being born on a New Moon, on Christmas Day, or on Friday the thirteenth.

- It is thought that a werewolf undergoes the change from a human form to a wolflike beast only under a full moon.

Glossary

ambush (AM-bush) A trap in which people hide and lie in wait to attack by surprise.

ancient (AYN-shent) Very old, from a long time ago.

attacks (uh-TAKS) Attempts to hurt someone or something.

chapel (CHA-pel) A small church.

creature (KREE-chur) A person or animal.

escort (ES-kort) To go with someone to give him or her protection or honor.

funerals (FYOON-rulz) The services held when burying the dead.

peasants (PEH-zents) People who farm small areas of land.

praised (PRAYZD) Said nice things about someone.

prey (PRAY) An animal that is hunted by another animal for food.

regret (rih-GRET) To feel sorry about having done something.

terror (TER-ur) Being very afraid.

vowed (VOWD) Made a very important promise.

Index

Web Sites

Due to the changing nature of Internet links, PowerKids Press has developed an online list of Web sites related to the subject of this book. This site is updated regularly. Please use this link to access the list:

www.powerkidslinks.com/mons/wolves/